Savage Sharks

Lynn Huggins-Cooper

Smart Apple Media

First published in 2005 by Franklin Watts
96 Leonard Street, London EC2A 4XD

Franklin Watts Australia
Level 17/207 Kent Street, Sydney NSW 2000

Editor: Jennifer Schofield
Jacket designer and Art director: Peter Scoulding
Designer: Jay Young
Picture researcher: Diana Morris

Acknowledgements:
Kelvin Aitkin/Still Pictures: 15, 19t. Fred Bavendam/FLPA: front cover cl. Tobias Bernard/OSF: 21.
David Fleetham/OSF: 20. Richard Herrman/OSF: 18–19. Klaus Jost/Image Quest Marine: 23.
Klaus Jost/Still Pictures: front cover r, 6. Frans Lanting/FLPA: front cover bl, 29. Doug Perrine/
Still Pictures: 11. Jeffrey L. Rotman/Still Pictures: 4–5, 7, 8, 9, 13, 16, 25. Masa Ushioda/Image
Quest Marine: 14, 17. James D. Watt/Image Quest Marine: 1, 10, 12, 22, 24, 26, 27, 28.

Published in the United States by Smart Apple Media
2140 Howard Drive West, North Mankato, Minnesota 56003

Printed in the United States of America

Library of Congress Cataloging-in-Publication Data

Huggins-Cooper, Lynn.
Savage sharks / by Lynn Huggins-Cooper.
p. cm. — (Killer nature)
ISBN-13 : 978-1-58340-933-6
1. Sharks—Juvenile literature. I. Title.

QL638.9.H84 2006
597.3—dc22   2005052052

9 8 7 6 5 4 3 2 1

Contents

Savage sharks

Sharks are the number one marine predator. They have been around since dinosaurs walked the planet. Sharks are admired by many people for their streamlined bodies and great swimming skills. However, many others see sharks as beasts from their worst nightmares.

Shark facts

There are 350 different kinds of sharks. Sharks are known as cartilaginous fish because their skeletons are made of cartilage rather than bone. These large fish are great survivors. They can go six weeks between meals and can replace teeth as they are damaged or lost. As a tooth is lost, another moves forward to replace it. Sharks can have an amazing 30,000 teeth in a lifetime!

Man-eating beasts

While some people take their chances by entering shark-infested waters in cages, most people are petrified of sharks. But the chances of actually being killed by one are quite small. Every year, more people are killed by jellyfish than by sharks. And sharks are at risk themselves. Fishermen kill about 100 million sharks every year—endangering the shark population.

Friend or foe?

But how can you tell whether a shark is harmless or a man-eater? Which shark is the most vicious, and is it safe to swim on a coral reef? Read on to find out. It just might save your life one day!

Fearsome great whites

Great whites are one of the most feared kinds of sharks in the world. They have "starred" in several films about sharks, including *Jaws*.

They live almost everywhere, including the Atlantic, Indian, and Pacific Oceans, the Gulf of Mexico, and the Red and Mediterranean Seas.

Vital statistics

Great white sharks grow to an average length of 12 to 16 feet (3.7–4.9 m), with the females being larger than the males. The biggest great white was caught off the coast of Cuba in 1945. It was an amazing 21 feet (6.4 m) long and weighed a staggering 3.6 tons (3.3 t).

How they kill

These stealthy killers travel along the bottom of the ocean, looking for shapes on the surface. When a shark spots its prey, it attacks suddenly from below. It charges up toward the creature and crashes into it, taking a huge bite. The shark leaves its prey to die from loss of blood before returning to feed.

Lots of teeth

Great white sharks have about 3,000 teeth, arranged in rows. The back teeth move forward as the ones at the front are broken or worn down. Sharks use their razor-sharp teeth to bite their prey into chunks, which they swallow whole.

Fact!

The top half of a great white is gray. This camouflages it in dark water as it sneaks up on prey from below.

More about great whites

Survival

Great whites have been killed in huge numbers by sport fishermen who see catching a "man-eater" as exciting. As a result, great white sharks are becoming rare and are an endangered species. They are protected by laws in parts of the United States and in Namibia, South Africa, parts of Australia, and Malta.

Baby great whites

Great white sharks give birth to between 2 and 14 baby sharks, called pups. The pups measure about five feet (1.5 m) at birth. As soon as the young are born, they swim away from their mother.

The pups grow 10 inches (25 cm) each year until they are fully grown at the age of 10. Since great whites have young only every other year, it is hard for their numbers to increase and for the great white population to grow.

Encounters with people

Great whites may be the most feared kind of shark—but is their reputation as man-eaters fair? In the 1990s, they were responsible for only 60 of the 480 shark attacks worldwide. As a result of great white bites, 11 people died. Although this sounds like a lot and is enough to make some people avoid the surf, it should be remembered that more people are killed by dogs each year than have been killed by great whites in the last 100 years.

Fact!

Fish give off electrical charges when they breathe. Great whites feel these charges and use them to find prey.

Real-life story

In 1963, Rodney Fox was viciously attacked by a great white. Rodney suffered life-threatening injuries. His abdomen was fully exposed, with all of the ribs on his left-hand side broken. His diaphragm was punctured, his lung ripped open, his shoulder pierced, his spleen uncovered, and the main artery from his heart exposed. The tendons, fingers, and thumb on his right hand were all cut, and to this day, Rodney has part of a great white tooth in his wrist. Incredibly, he survived what is thought to be one of the world's worst attacks. Rodney now runs a museum in Adelaide, Australia, dedicated to great whites.

Terrifying tiger sharks

Tiger sharks get their name from the dark stripes across their back, which fade as they grow older.

They are found in tropical waters around the world and can live close to the shore and out in the open sea.

Vital statistics

Tiger sharks can grow up to an amazing 19.5 feet (6 m) long, but they are usually 10 to 13 feet (3–4 m) long. These beasts have a great sense of smell and can pick up tiny traces of blood in the water. Like great whites, they can sense movements, enabling them to hunt in dark or murky water.

In a tiger's tummy

Tiger sharks are sometimes called the garbage cans of the sea because they swallow just about anything, including tires, car license plates, and shoes. They can push their stomach through their mouth, which allows them to "spit" out any undigestible food.

Real-life story

In 1935, a vicious tiger shark caught off the coast of Australia regurgitated, or spat out, a person's arm. The arm was identified by a tattoo, but, unfortunately, the rest of the body has never been found.

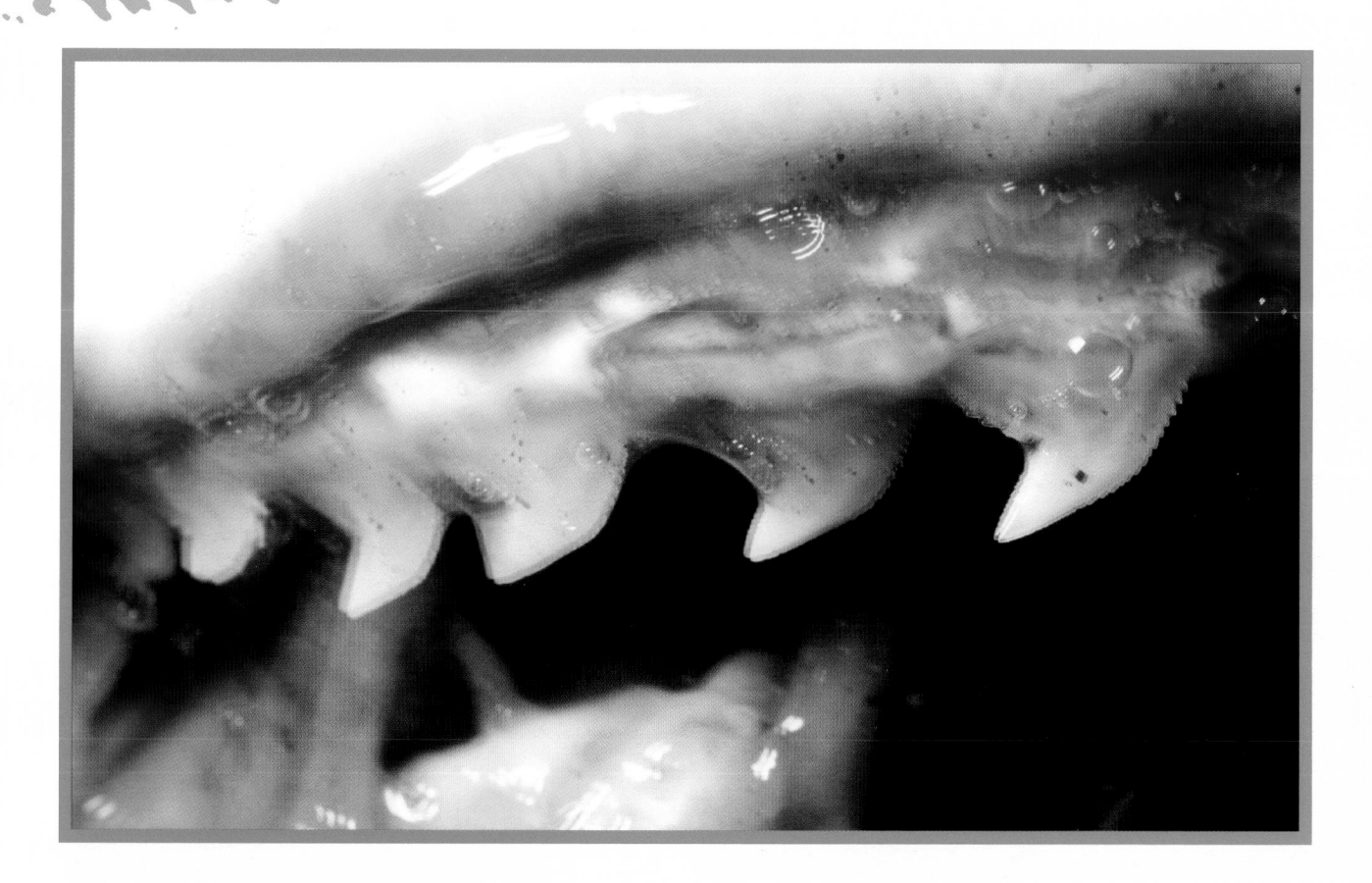

Encounters with people

Tiger sharks are some of the most feared sharks in tropical waters. They are aggressive and are curious about people in the water, making them one of the three main shark species known to attack humans.

How they kill

When tiger sharks find their prey, they swim around it in circles, nudging it with their broad snout. The sharks then attack with their vicious teeth and swallow the victim in chunks.

More about tiger sharks

Survival

Tiger sharks are hunted by sport fishermen, and their fins are popular as food in some parts of the world. But they are not an endangered species.

Unlike some sharks, female tiger sharks give birth to large numbers of pups. The young grow quickly, which ensures their survival.

Baby tiger sharks

Tiger sharks have between 10 and 80 pups at a time. The mother does not lay eggs. Instead, she carries the babies for nine months before they are born.

When they are born, the young are independent and can swim. They also have a full set of teeth and can hunt as soon as they are born.

When tiger sharks attack

These terrifying sharks are not afraid of people. One report tells of a shark that attacked two men and a woman on a life raft. The shark killed and ate one man, then came back later and dragged the woman off the raft and killed her. The second man escaped and was very lucky not to be harmed.

Small but deadly

Tiger sharks have a small but deadly enemy— the puffer fish. The sharks think that the puffers are food and eat them. The small fish then inflate themselves in the sharks' throat. This keeps water from passing over the sharks' gills, which eventually kills the sharks.

Traveling blue sharks

Blue sharks are common and have one of the widest ranges of all sharks. They are found in the tropical and temperate waters of the Atlantic and Pacific Oceans and the Arabian and Mediterranean Seas.

Blue sharks are excellent swimmers and can swim long distances. A blue shark that was tagged in New York was caught 16 months later off the coast of Brazil—that is a swim of more than 3,730 miles (6,000 km)!

Vital statistics
On average, blue sharks measure 8 to 10 feet (2.5–3 m) long. The largest of these great swimmers can grow up to nearly 13 feet (4 m) in length and can weigh up to 550 pounds (250 kg).

Whale watchers

Blue sharks race through groups of squid with their mouth wide open, eating many of these tiny creatures at a time. They also like to eat whale carcasses found floating in the water.

Fishermen often encounter blue sharks biting at whale carcasses in such a frenzy that they don't notice when the fishermen hit them with huge spades!

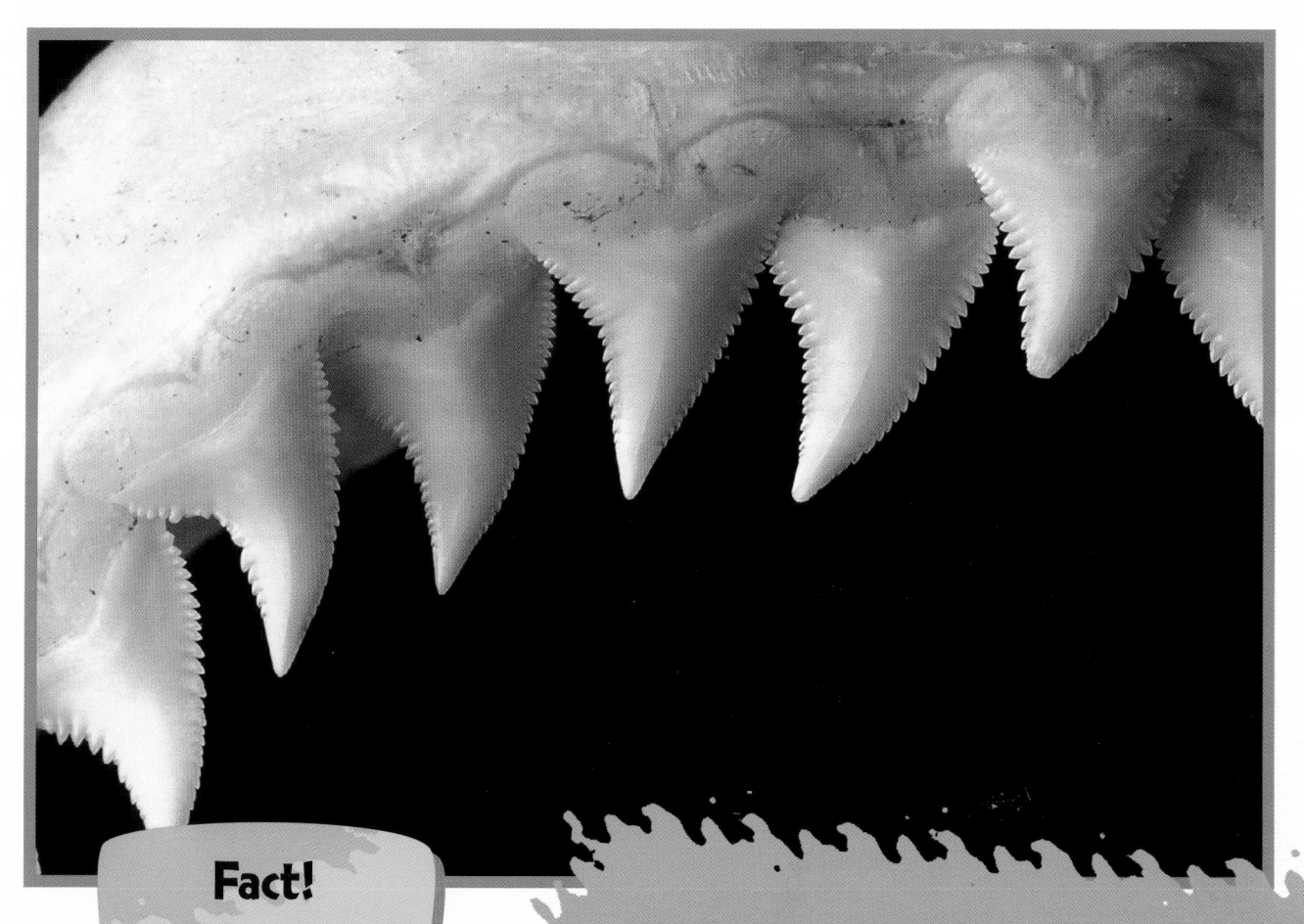

Fact!

Blue sharks have a thin membrane over their eyes that helps to protect their eyes from damage during an attack.

How they kill

Blue sharks eat mainly small fish and squid. Their teeth are serrated like bread knives. This helps them to catch and hold on to the slippery fish. Like many other types of sharks, they have several rows of teeth that move forward to replace the old teeth as they break or are lost.

More about blue sharks

Survival

Blue sharks are quite common, but many are caught by fishermen around the world. Numbers could fall as a result of overfishing and the accidental capture of sharks in commercial fishing nets.

Baby blue sharks

Female blue sharks give birth to live young that have hatched from eggs inside the mother's body. Until they are born, the pups are fed by a yolk sack. The pup shown above was born early and is still attached to its sack.

There can be up to 130 pups in a litter, but normally there are between 25 and 50. The pups are 15.5 to 20 inches (40–51 cm) long when they are born.

Encounters with people

Although blue sharks feed mainly on small squid, they are dangerous and have been known to attack people and boats. Most of the attacks are on fishermen who accidentally catch the blue sharks in their nets.

There are also recorded attacks on divers and people stranded in the ocean. However, blue sharks are less aggressive than many other types of sharks, and few fatalities from blue shark attacks have been recorded.

Fact!

Every year, great white sharks attack 15 times as many divers as blue sharks.

Speedy shortfin makos

Shortfin makos are beautiful sharks, with deep blue backs and snowy white bellies.

They are found around the world in temperate and tropical seas.

Vital statistics

Shortfin makos can weigh up to 1,000 pounds (455 kg) and can grow up to 12 feet (3.7 m) long. They are incredibly fast swimmers and can reach speeds of up to 30 miles (50 km) per hour. Terrifyingly, they can use their speed to launch themselves up to 40 feet (12 m) out of the water!

How they kill

Shortfin makos hunt other fast-swimming fish that travel in large groups, or schools, such as tuna, herring, and mackerel. The sharks have long, needle-sharp teeth that help them to grab and stab the slippery fish.

Encounters with people

Shortfin makos are large and dangerous, with powerful jaws and very sharp teeth. Most of their attacks are on fishermen. The sharks are seen as a "prize catch" because they fight hard when they are caught. If people did not try to catch them, there would be few injuries, since makos live far out in the open ocean where divers and swimmers rarely venture.

Baby makos

When they are still in the womb, the more-developed, stronger baby makos will eat other, less-developed pups. As a result, shortfin makos have small litters of between 10 and 12 pups. The pups are about two feet (.6 m) long when they are born.

Curious gray reef sharks

Gray reef sharks are one of the most common types of reef sharks. These stream-lined fish are found in tropical waters such as the Pacific and Indian Oceans.

In the daytime, schools of 20 to 100 gray reef sharks gather and swim across reefs and lagoons. They are curious and like to investigate when divers enter the water.

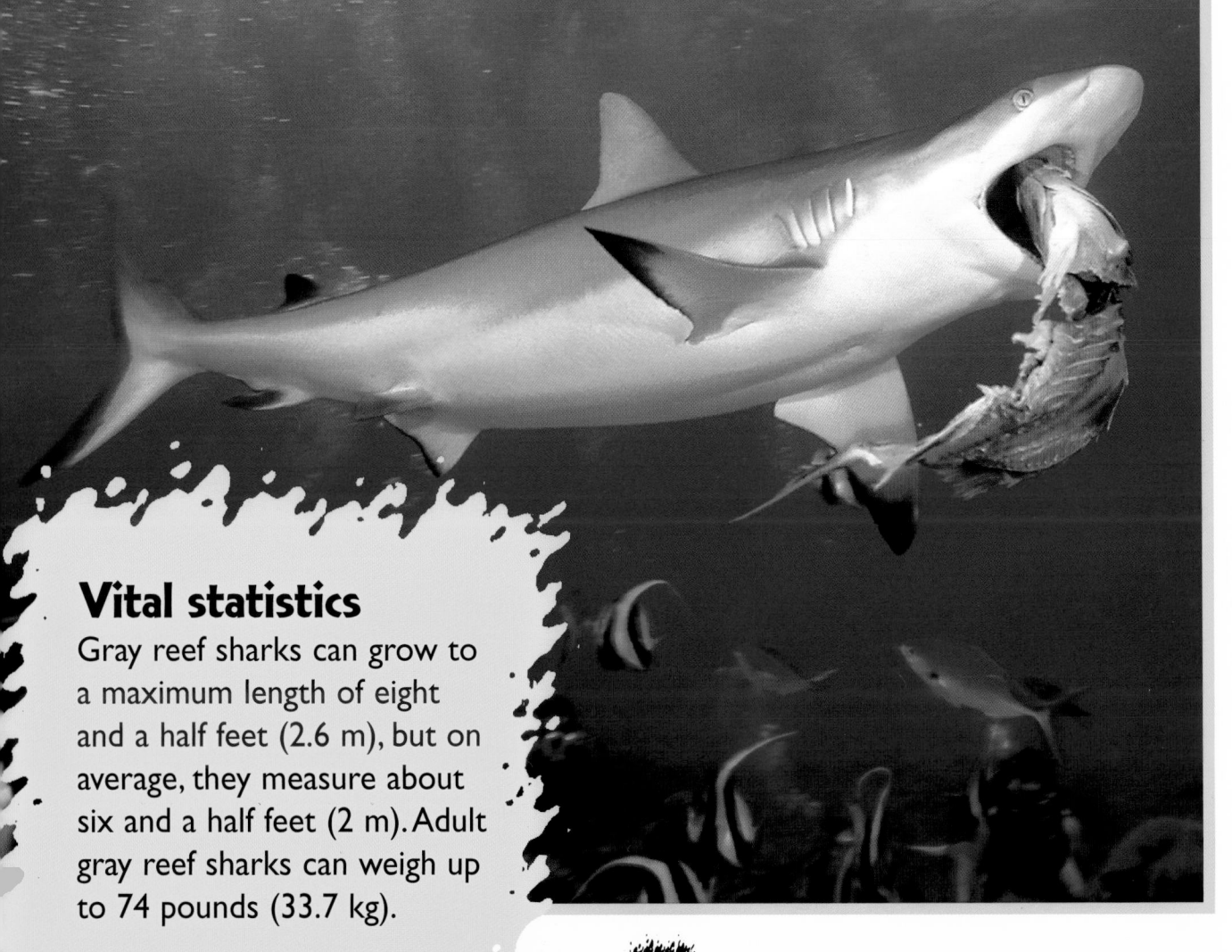

Vital statistics
Gray reef sharks can grow to a maximum length of eight and a half feet (2.6 m), but on average, they measure about six and a half feet (2 m). Adult gray reef sharks can weigh up to 74 pounds (33.7 kg).

How they kill

Gray reef sharks feed mainly at night. They eat fish and different types of seafood such as squid, octopus, crab, shrimp, and lobster. Sometimes a school of gray reef sharks will work together to ambush schools of small fish. They attack the fish suddenly from below.

Real-life story

A spear fisherman had caught a fish when a gray reef shark shot toward him. The shark and the diver wrestled together, the shark biting the diver's arm and the diver punching the shark's head. The shark bit the man's arm to the bone before it swam off, and the diver scrambled out of the water.

Baby gray reef sharks

Gray reef sharks give birth to live young. There are between one and six pups in each litter. The young sharks measure 18 to 24 inches (45–60 cm) when they are born.

Deadly bull sharks

Bull sharks are found in tropical and subtropical seas. They also swim in warm rivers such as the Amazon, the Mississippi, the Zambezi, and the Ganges, and are found in freshwater lakes such as Nicaragua in Central America.

These fierce sharks can swim in water that is less than three feet (.9 m) deep. Many researchers think a bull shark was the legendary Jersey man-eater—the shark that killed several swimmers in Mattawan Creek, New Jersey, in 1916.

Vital statistics

Bull sharks can be up to 11 feet (3.4 m) long, with the females being larger than the males. The sharks can weigh up to 500 pounds (230 kg).

What's for dinner?

Almost everything has been found in the stomachs of bull sharks, from bicycle tires to human remains. These sharks also eat bony fish, rays, and other sharks—sometimes even other bull sharks—as well as sea turtles, dolphins, and birds.

How they kill

These dangerous sharks hunt alone. Although they are often thought of as sluggish sharks, when bull sharks attack, they can be surprisingly quick. Since bull sharks prefer to hunt in murky water, they can easily mistake a person for prey.

Encounters with people

Bull sharks are extremely dangerous to humans, and it is thought that they are responsible for some of the attacks blamed on great whites.

In KwaZulu-Natal, South Africa, bull sharks are caught four times more often than other sharks in the nets that protect swimming areas on beaches.

More about bull sharks

Real-life story

In 2001, eight-year-old Jessie Arbogast was playing in about two feet (.6 m) of water when a deadly bull shark attacked him. The vicious shark tore off his arm before Jessie's uncle managed to pull the shark onto the beach, where park rangers shot it. Fortunately, Jessie survived the attack, and surgeons were able to stitch his arm back on.

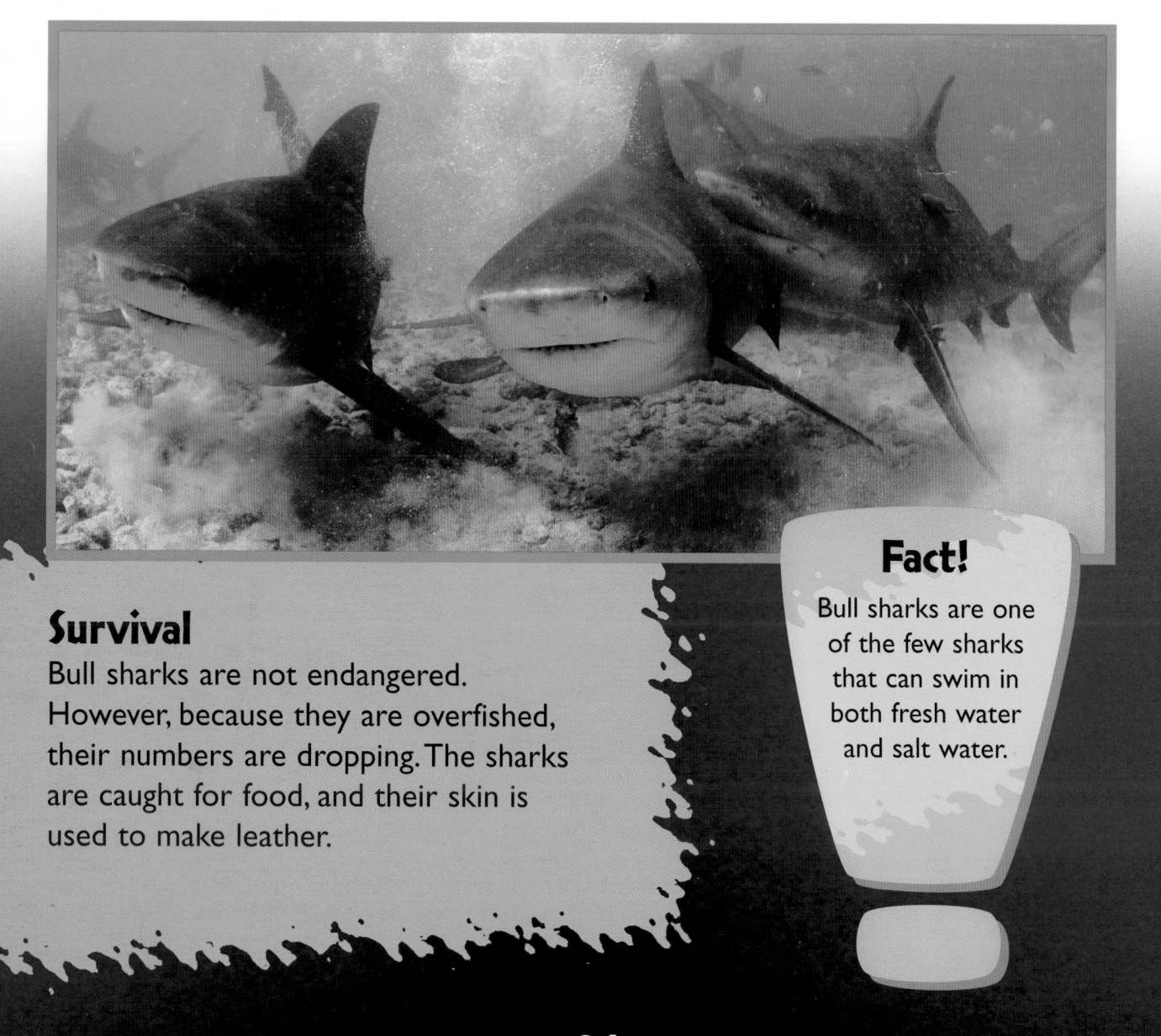

Survival

Bull sharks are not endangered. However, because they are overfished, their numbers are dropping. The sharks are caught for food, and their skin is used to make leather.

Fact!

Bull sharks are one of the few sharks that can swim in both fresh water and salt water.

Baby bull sharks

Bull sharks give birth to between 1 and 13 pups in each litter. When they are born, the pups are between 21.5 and 31.5 inches (55–80 cm) long, but they grow slowly. The pups are usually born in murky water in areas where salt water and fresh water meet—at the mouth of a river, for example.

Unique hammerheads

Great hammerhead sharks are easily recognized by their T-shaped heads. They are found in the Pacific Ocean, the Gulf of Mexico, and the Caribbean and Red Seas. These unique looking sharks swim around coral reefs and close to the shore in shallow water.

Vital statistics

On average, great hammerhead sharks are between 13 and 16 feet (4–5 m) from their snout to their tail.

The largest great hammerheads measure up to 20 feet (6.1 m) and weigh about 2.5 tons (2.3 t).

Baby hammerheads

Great hammerhead eggs hatch inside the female's body. There are usually between 12 and 20 pups in each litter. When the pups are born, they are 19.5 to 27.5 inches (50–70 cm) long. Newborn pups have rounder heads than the adults, but this changes as they grow and develop their "hammer" shape.

Encounters with people

Great hammerheads attack people, but not in the same numbers as great whites, bull sharks, and tiger sharks. The International Shark Attack File has recorded 21 unprovoked attacks, with 2 resulting in death. The File ranks hammerheads seventh among the sharks most dangerous to humans.

How they kill

Great hammerheads eat large fish, squid, octopuses, stingrays, and other sharks. These unusual sharks swim along the ocean floor and swing their hammer-shaped head from side to side to find their prey.

Fact!

Hammerheads' skin is used for leather, their liver oil is used to make vitamins, and their bodies are ground to make fish meal.

Toothy sand tiger sharks

Sand tiger sharks are found in the waters off South America, South Africa, India, China, Japan, and Australia. They live in sandy coastal waters, shallow bays, reefs, and estuaries. These sharks can adjust their buoyancy by gulping air and burping as they swim underwater.

Vital statistics

Sand tigers are one of the scariest looking kinds of sharks. They can grow up to about 10 feet (3 m) long from nose to tail. Added to their size, they have a huge mouth filled with teeth, which makes them look incredibly fierce. In South Africa, they are called ragged-tooth sharks, or "raggies."

Baby sand tigers

Female sand tigers give birth to one or two live pups. The female produces 16 to 23 eggs, but the hatched pups feed on the other eggs while they are still inside the female. The pups are up to three feet (.9 m) long when they are born. This large size increases their chances of survival to adulthood.

When sand tigers attack

Sand tiger sharks rarely attack, but they will if they are provoked. When spear fishermen stab fish, the scent of blood attracts sand tigers, resulting in the fishermen being bitten.

At public aquariums, sand tigers may become very fat from overfeeding. They are fed constantly to keep them from attacking other fish in the tanks—or the aquarium staff!

Survival

Sand tiger sharks are often killed, perhaps because of their threatening appearance. As a result, their numbers are falling. Several countries, including the U.S., Australia, and New Guinea, have given the shark protection.

How they kill

Sand tiger sharks eat fish, small sharks, squid, crabs, and lobsters. Sometimes a school of sand tigers hunts and feeds together. The sharks surround schools of prey fish and herd them together so they can be eaten easily.

Key words

Ambush
A surprise attack from a hidden place.

Buoyancy
The ability of something to float.

Camouflage
Special colors or markings found
on plants and animals that help them
remain hidden.

Cartilage
The strong, rubbery substance
that a shark's skeleton is made
from. Cartilage also gives human
noses and ears their shape.

Commercial fishermen
Fishermen who catch fish and sell
them to make money.

Endangered species
A group of living things in danger
of dying out completely.

Estuaries
The wide mouths of rivers where
they meet the sea.

Fresh water
The water found in rivers, lakes, and
streams.

Gills
The parts of the body fish use for
breathing.

Marine
Anything to do with or in the sea.

Membrane
A thin layer that protects organs.

Overfishing
Catching so many fish that their
numbers fall.

Predators
Animals that hunt and eat other animals.

Prey
Animals hunted by other animals
for food.

Reefs
Areas of coral in warm, shallow sea
waters.

Regurgitate
To bring something back into the mouth
after swallowing it.

School
A group of fish of the same species.

Serrated
When something is sharp, jagged, and pointy.

Shark nets
The nets placed off the coastline of popular swimming and surfing beaches. The nets prevent the sharks from getting too close to swimmers and surfers.

Spear fishermen
A deep-sea sport in which divers swim close enough to fish to kill them with a type of spear.

Species
A group of closely related animals that can breed with each other.

Sport fishermen
Fishermen who fish for fun.

Streamlined
When an animal has a smooth shape to help it move easily through the air or water.

Temperate
When something is neither too hot nor too cold.

Tropical
To do with the area in or around the tropics that has a warm climate.

Web links

http://www.nationalgeographic.com/ kids/creature_feature/0206/sharks.html
A *National Geographic* feature on sharks.

http://www.sdnhm.org/kids/sharks
Shark school for kids! Features lots of fun-filled shark activities and puzzles.

http://dsc.discovery.com/convergence/ sharkweek/quizzes/quizzes.html
Quizzes to test your shark knowledge.

http://www.enchantedlearning.com/ subjects/sharks
Lots of information on sharks, things to make, and pictures to download and color.

http://www.flmnh.ufl.edu/fish/kids/ Avoid/avoid.htm
A special kids' feature on how to avoid shark attacks.

http://www.howstuffworks.com/ shark.htm
Lots of facts and figures about sharks.

Note to parents:
Every effort has been made to ensure that the Web sites in this book are suitable for children, that they are of the highest educational value, and that they contain no inappropriate or offensive material. However, due to the nature of the Internet, it is impossible to guarantee that the contents of these sites will not be altered. We strongly advise that Internet access be supervised by a responsible adult.

Index